KICK, JUMP, CHEER!
CHEERLEADING TRYOUTS

BY SARA GREEN

BELLWETHER MEDIA • MINNEAPOLIS, MN

Jump into the cockpit and take flight with Pilot Books. Your journey will take you on high-energy adventures as you learn about all that is wild, weird, fascinating, and fun!

This edition first published in 2012 by Bellwether Media, Inc.

No part of this publication may be reproduced in whole or in part without written permission of the publisher.
For information regarding permission, write to Bellwether Media, Inc., Attention: Permissions Department,
5357 Penn Avenue South, Minneapolis, MN 55419.

Library of Congress Cataloging-in-Publication Data
Green, Sara, 1964–
 Cheerleading tryouts / by Sara Green.
    p. cm. — (Pilot books: kick, jump, cheer!)
 Includes bibliographical references and index.
 Summary: "Engaging images accompany information about cheerleading tryouts. The combination of high-interest subject matter and narrative text is intended for students in grades 3 through 7"—Provided by publisher.
 ISBN 978-1-60014-651-0 (hardcover : alk. paper)
 1. Cheerleading—Juvenile literature. I. Title.
 LB3635.G746 2011
 791.6'4—dc22   2011011671

Printed in the United States of America, North Mankato, MN.

080111   1187

CONTENTS

LOVE TO CHEER!

Do you enjoy watching cheerleaders **rally** crowds and perform exciting **routines**? Do you know a lot of **chants** and **cheers** by heart? Do you have a positive attitude? If so, you might make a great cheerleader! Every cheerleader must go through a **tryout** to make a **squad**. At a tryout, you perform cheerleading skills in front of coaches and squad **captains**. They invite cheerleaders with the best skills to join the squad.

It's not easy to earn a spot on a cheerleading squad. A lot of people try out for a limited number of spots. The key to a great tryout is to be prepared. As soon as you decide to try out, it's time to start mastering basic cheerleading skills. Your hard work and commitment will pay off at your tryout. You will be able to show your spirit with confidence!

PREPARING FOR THE TRYOUT

The first step toward becoming a cheerleader is to get into shape. Cheerleaders need strength, **flexibility**, and **stamina**. The coach at school or a trainer at a local gym can help you create a workout plan. Exercises such as push-ups and pull-ups strengthen your muscles. Stretching every day increases your flexibility and helps you avoid injuries. To build stamina, jump rope or dance to upbeat music. Biking, jogging, and swimming are other great activities that get you into shape. Eat healthy foods and get plenty of rest to stay strong and energetic. A healthy body will help you do your best at the tryout.

You will have to perform a variety of skills at your tryout. They include cheers, chants, and jumps. You might also show off your dance and **tumbling** moves. The cheerleading coach can give you a list of the skills you will be expected to perform. Begin practicing these skills well ahead of time. You may need several months to get ready for your tryout. During this time, try to attend performances by the squad you want to join. You will get an idea of the moves you should practice for the tryout. If the squad performs tumbling moves, you could take gymnastics classes. If the routines include dance moves, sign up for dance classes to get into the rhythm.

Be sure you learn the basics before your tryout. Remember to keep your movements sharp and clean!

FEET TOGETHER
Stand up straight and put your shoulders back. Keep your feet together.

"L"
Form the letter "L" with your arms. Keep each hand in a fist. Point one arm straight up and the other arm to the side.

BLADE
Open your hands flat. Keep your fingers together. Extend your arms straight out to each side without bending your wrists.

BOW AND ARROW
Make a fist with each hand. Extend one arm straight out to the side. Bend the other arm at the elbow so that the fist is touching your chest.

Jumps are also important to practice before your tryout. Cheerleaders often jump at the same time during games. They perform a variety of different jumps depending on their skill level. Flexibility is the key to jumping well. Be sure to stretch your muscles before and after practicing jumps. The more you practice, the easier it will be to jump to the top at your tryout!

These are some of the most common cheerleading jumps:

TUCK Make fists with your hands and jump straight into the air. Keep your feet together and bring your knees toward your chest. Raise your arms in a "V" shape.

HURDLER
Jump and extend one leg straight out in front of you. Bend the other leg and tuck it behind you.

toe touch

HERKIE
Kick one leg straight out to the side as you jump. Bend the other leg so your knee faces the ground.

TOE TOUCH
Jump and spread your legs wide. Reach your right hand toward your right foot and your left hand toward your left foot.

COMMITMENT AND RESPONSIBILITY

Most cheerleading coaches schedule a meeting a few weeks before tryouts. Anyone who wants to try out should attend. At this meeting, you may ask coaches and captains questions. They will explain the responsibilities that come with being a cheerleader. Cheerleaders are expected to perform at every game and promote spirit, enthusiasm, and good **sportsmanship**. Cheerleading is a big commitment. Cheerleaders often practice every day after school. They also plan **pep rallies** and other activities to raise school spirit.

Cheerleaders are role models for younger children. They are expected to show good behavior at school and in their communities. Many schools require cheerleaders to get good grades and help with fundraising events. It's important that you understand what it means to join a squad before you try out.

PRACTICE WEEK

Cheerleading squads often schedule a practice week before tryouts. During practice week, coaches and squad captains teach students the routines they will perform at tryouts. The coaches pay close attention to everyone's attitude. They notice who works hard, respects others, and is enthusiastic. If you show a positive attitude, the coaches will remember you on tryout day.

It's important to spend time every day practicing on your own. Ask an experienced cheerleader to watch you practice. You can get feedback on how to improve your moves. You could also practice in front of a mirror. Remember to keep your arm and leg movements sharp. Use a clear, strong voice when you practice chants and cheers. Don't forget to smile!

PRACTICE TIP: If you have a video camera, ask someone to record you practicing. Watch the video to see what you need to work on.

TRYOUT DAY

When tryout day arrives, you will perform for the coaches and captains. They will give you scores for your moves, jumps, spirit, voice, and overall performance. Show them your spirit right from the start. When you make your entrance, run onto the floor yelling "Let's Go!" or "We're Number One!" The coaches and captains will ask you to perform specific cheers, chants, and jumps. You will also perform a dance routine with a partner or the entire group.

Sometimes cheerleaders are asked to perform an original cheer. Have a creative, exciting cheer ready just in case. If you have outstanding tumbling skills, be sure to include tumbling in your cheer. Do you project your voice better than anyone you know? Let them hear your clear, strong voice. Remember to make eye contact and keep your movements sharp. Your confidence will set you apart!

It is normal to be nervous on tryout day. Get to your tryout early so that you have time to stretch. Take deep breaths to calm your nerves. When it's your turn, enter the gym with confidence. If you make a mistake during your tryout, keep going as if nothing happened. The coaches and captains know you are nervous. It is common for people to make mistakes. You will impress them if you recover from a mistake with a smile on your face.

If you don't make the squad, talk to the coach about what you can do to improve. The coach will remember your commitment and desire to be on the squad at next year's tryout. You will have a year to improve your skills. Make time every day to stretch and practice. After the next tryout, you might find yourself on the squad!

CHECKLIST FOR TRYOUT DAY

⭐ Wear comfortable clothes in team colors
⭐ Wear sturdy athletic shoes
⭐ Pull long hair away from your face with a hair band
⭐ Remove all jewelry
⭐ Wear very little makeup
⭐ Bring a water bottle and a snack
⭐ Have all forms filled out and ready to hand in
⭐ Smile!

GO FOR IT!

Trying out for a cheerleading squad is both exciting and scary. The secret is to be prepared. As soon as you decide to try out, start practicing. Perfect your current skills and learn new ones. Get into shape by working on your strength, flexibility, and stamina. Work out with a friend to **motivate** each other for the tryout. You can give each other tips and encouragement.

Remember that cheerleading is a big commitment. You want to be sure that it is right for you. If you have any questions about tryouts or cheerleading in general, ask the coach or current cheerleaders. Go into your tryout with confidence and enthusiasm. Your skills, smile, and positive attitude will impress everyone. You are on your way to becoming a cheerleader. Have fun!

GLOSSARY

captains—the leaders of a sports team; cheerleading captains help coaches lead practices and plan events.

chants—short, repetitive phrases yelled during a game

cheers—long phrases yelled during routines; jumps and stunts often go along with cheers.

flexibility—the ability to stretch and move the body with ease

motivate—to encourage to do something

pep rallies—gatherings held before sporting events to boost school spirit and encourage sports teams

rally—to stir up and encourage enthusiasm

routines—sequences of moves that cheerleaders practice and perform

sportsmanship—showing fair play, respect for others, and grace whether winning or losing

squad—a group of cheerleaders that works together as a team

stamina—the ability to do something for a long time

tryout—an event where people perform skills for coaches and captains in order to make a team

tumbling—gymnastics skills such as cartwheels and handsprings; many cheerleading squads use tumbling in their routines.

TO LEARN MORE

At the Library

Gruber, Beth. *Cheerleading for Fun*. Minneapolis, Minn.: Compass Point Books, 2004.

Jones, Jen. *Cheer Tryouts: Making the Cut*. Mankato, Minn.: Capstone Press, 2006.

Mullarkey, Lisa. *Cheerleading Tryouts and Competitions*. Berkeley Heights, N.J.: Enslow Publishers, 2011.

On the Web

Learning more about cheerleading is as easy as 1, 2, 3.

1. Go to www.factsurfer.com.

2. Enter "cheerleading" into the search box.

3. Click the "Surf" button and you will see a list of related Web sites.

With factsurfer.com, finding more information is just a click away.

INDEX

The images in this book are reproduced through the courtesy of: Rubberball/Mike Kemp/ Getty Images, front cover, p. 13; James Hajjar, pp. 5, 21; Jim Cayer/Cayer's Sports Action Photography, pp. 7, 9, 11, 17; Tom Carter/Age Fotostock, p. 15; Erik Isakson/Photolibrary, p. 19